DS

The Simple Art of

Celtic

Calligraphy

The Simple Art of Celtic Calligraphy

20 step-by-step projects and essential techniques

Fiona Graham-Flynn

CICO BOOKS

LONDON NEW YORK

Published in 2008 by CICO Books
an imprint of Ryland Peters & Small
20–21 Jockey's Fields, London WC1R 4BW

www.cicobooks.co.uk

10 9 8 7 6 5 4 3 2 1

Text copyright © Fiona Graham-Flynn 2008
Design and photography copyright © CICO
Books 2008

A CIP catalogue record for this book is available
from the British Library.

ISBN-13: 978 1 906094 68 3

Printed in China

Editor: Robin Gurdon
Designer: Ian Midson
Photographer: Geoff Dann

Contents

Introduction

The beauty of Celtic calligraphy was captured in the great manuscript works of the Middle Ages. With this book, you can learn to create your own pieces of art, inspired by works such as the majestic Books of Kells.

The ancient art of calligraphy evolved into the form we recognize today, the Uncial script, with the Roman writing of their majuscule, or capital, letters. The English and Irish style of majuscule letters, known as Insular style, that developed into the Uncial alphabet was first seen in the sixth and seventh centuries. By the eighth century it had been joined by the miniscule, or lower-case, letters of the Half-uncial alphabet with their characteristic rounded form.

A modern rendering of the Cross of Enniaun

In these early centuries all writing of note was created by monks known as scribes. Living in monasteries across northern England, Scotland and Ireland, it was their job to create the holy books used by the early Christian Church in the centuries before the advent of printing. One such monastery was located on the remote island now known as Holy Island, just off the Northumbrian coast of England. It is here in the eighth century that the great work known as the Lindisfarne Gospels was written, using an Uncial script with large illuminated pages of vivid colour.

The tiny Scottish island of Iona, founded by the Irish monk St Columba, was to become the birthplace of more acclaimed manuscripts in the ninth century. Here the famous Book of Kells, also a set of the four Gospels, was inscribed. Ireland, too, has produced beautiful manuscripts such as the Book of Durrow and Armagh.

Born in Scotland and now living in England, I have been a calligrapher for 28 years and have always been drawn back to the calligraphy and art inspired by those amazing Celtic scribes. The scripts were written with a quill pen cut from the flight feathers of a goose or swan, not on paper but on vellum which was made from calf skin. Every scribe had a unique writing hand, and their personality can sometimes be seen in the little notes that they left in the margins of the pages – how they were tired of writing or how their hands were cold. Parts of these books were decorated with what are known as carpet pages. Where pages had no text they were instead covered with patterns and shapes designed with spirals, interlacing knotwork, key patterns and beautiful colour work.

The manuscript books were written in different ways. Sometimes one scribe alone would write and illustrate the pages throughout a whole book in what could turn out to

The Book of Kells was written in the early ninth century. This page of beautiful Half-uncial script is decorated with illuminated letters and stunning zoomorphic decoration.

Written a century before the Book of Kells in the north of England,
the Lindisfarne Gospels included illuminated pages of cursive capitals
decorated with intricate, vividly coloured designs.

be a lifetime's work. In other books, one scribe skilled in calligraphy would write the text, passing it on to another monk who would illuminate and embellish the pages with coloured pigments.

This book will endeavour to feed your imagination with 20 simple inventive projects. You will be amazed at what you can achieve using the step-by-step instructions and easy-to-follow pictures. Once finished, each project can be kept or can be given as presents to friends, family, children and grandchildren.

Enjoy the challenge and have fun mastering the art of Celtic calligraphy!

MATERIALS

Although a calligrapher's array of equipment can look daunting, you can start with just a single pen, some black calligraphy ink and plain cartridge paper. As you become more practised, enjoy finding those new materials that will enhance your calligraphy.

Materials

The beauty of calligraphy can only be properly appreciated if it is created with the right materials. The pens and nibs must allow the letters to be written smoothly and crisply, paper needs to be beautiful to touch and not smudge carefully crafted wording, inks should be deep, black and true and brushes must be fine enough to allow the finest decoration to be added. Start with a few basic pieces and gradually build up your collection of materials as your calligraphy improves.

The basic materials you will need to start practising calligraphy are paper, pens and inks. Start with just a few items and discover the products that you feel most comfortable using. As well as the basic writing tools you should also have a supply of tracing paper, some soft and hard pencils, a ruler, an eraser and a fine line black pen. Most imporant of all, though, is to ensure you have a comfortable, even drawing board to work at.

Papers

There are many calligraphy papers available – the best being smooth paper called 'hot-pressed' which will take the ink very well. Vegetable parchment papers are also nice to work with and they come in a variety of colours, from white to deep colours.

Watercolour and canson papers and thin card can be white through to deep shades and they give an interesting textured look to the writing. Handmade papers are also nice to use, although some can be porous, which makes it more difficult to write on them smoothly.

More exotic papers include goatskin parchment paper which comes in two weights and is sold in ivory and cream colours. It has a smooth surface and is watermarked. Vellum and parchment hides are good if you are writing something special as they not only look beautiful but have a lovely feel when writing and mistakes can be easily scraped away.

Pens

A pen holder which can take many different nibs is the most common calligraphy tool. They can be made from natural wood, decorative colour-coated wood and plastic.

The most common nib is the straight chisel end nib which comes in a variety of sizes from 6, the smallest, to 0, the largest. A brass ink reservoir needs to be combined with this type of nib. Oblique nibs for left-handers are obtainable, too.

There are other nibs available that give different decorative writing strokes including pointed and double-ended. Multi-point nibs can also be interesting as they replicate 5 writing lines for every letter. There are also automatic pens where the nib and holder are in one. These tend to be larger in size and need to be filled with ink with a brush.

A useful pen to have is a fine point black pen. A draughtsman's drawing pen is best for fine line work as they can be bought in various size points. Metallic gold and silver pens of different point thicknesses are also useful.

Brushes

Of the many brushes available the best for fine brush work are red sable brushes on illumination. They come in various sizes – the 000, 0 and 1 are the most useful for this type of painting when a fine brush is needed. There are synthetic brushes too, but they do

My studio has plenty of natural light and lots of storage space for inks, paper and brushes. My collection of ink wells sits on the shelf by the radio.

not hold the paint in the bristles as well as sable brushes and they are not as flexible when applying the colour.

A size 3 or 4 nylon brush is fine for mixing paint and applying gouache paint to the nib.

Inks and colours

Inks play an important part in writing calligraphy. Black ink is the most common ink used. Chinese black ink is ideal as it is dense, black and retains a good consistency. Of the rest, waterproof coloured inks can be useful but they are usually thin and translucent. Pearlised inks add a metallic look and come in a variety of colours but they need to be constantly stirred while being used, as the metallic part of the liquid sinks to the bottom of the pot.

Gouache paint is a nice medium to use. It comes in many colours and can be mixed to produce many more. They are best used with a drop of liquid gum arabic and water to bind the colour.

Papers

Take care to work on suitable paper that shows off your calligraphy at its best. Some make the ink spread or soak it up dulling the quality of your writing, while others can show off the precision and clarity of a piece of calligraphy. As well as watercolour and hot-pressed papers, have a supply of practice paper, tracing paper and even pieces of vellum and parchment for those very special projects.

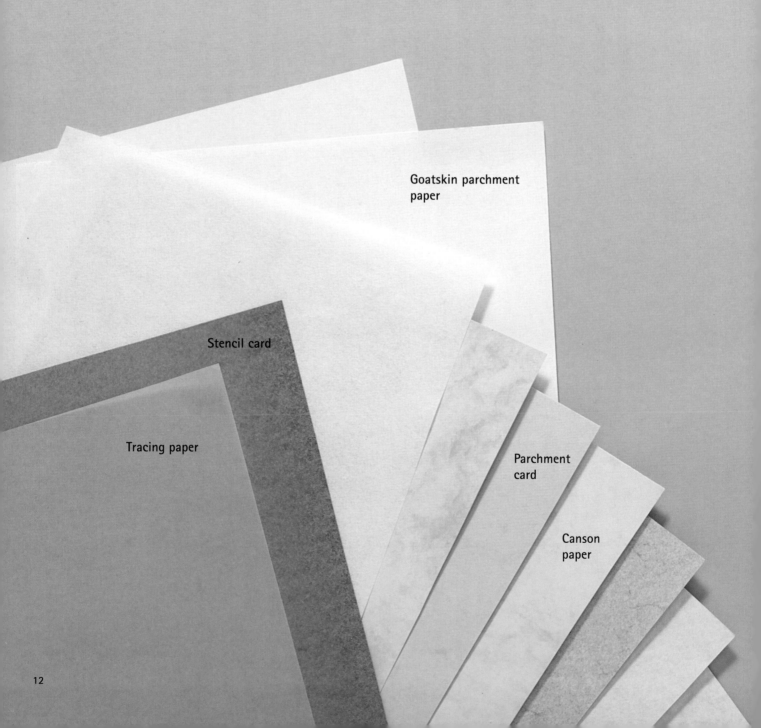

Goatskin parchment paper

Stencil card

Tracing paper

Parchment card

Canson paper

Cartridge paper

Coloured
textured
paper

Hot-pressed
coloured papers

Goatskin parchment

Vellum

Pens and Brushes

Using the calligrapher's pen, with its assorted nibs and reservoirs, the artist can create an incredible array of scripts and alphabets. Adding just a paintbrush, a fine line black pen and a pencil ensures there is no writing that cannot be created.

Calligraphy nibs

Copperplate and double-point nibs

Decorative pen holders

Pen holders with nibs and reservoirs

Multi-nibbed pen

Automatic pens

Metallic marker pen

Sable
paintbrushes

Gold marker
pen

Fine line black
marker pens

Stencilling brushes

Flat varnishing
brush

Chinagraph
pencil

Retractable
pencil

Double
pencils

15

Inks and Colours

The inks and colours create the textures of calligraphy. Starting with traditional black ink add coloured, metallic and even pearlized inks to your collection as well as gouache and enamel colours. Don't forget all the extra tools to make your calligraphy a success, from scissors and a ruler through to specialist items like the flexible curve.

Flexible curve

Compass

Pinking shears

Lino-cutting tool

Craft knife

Scissors

Eraser

Cutting board and rulers

Coloured waterproof ink

Palette

Water jar

Gouache colours

Gum arabic

Colour pencils

Enamel paints

Pearlescent ink

Gold calligraphy ink

Pearlized calligraphy ink

Silver calligraphy ink

Waterproof fabric paint

Chinese black ink

Coloured calligraphy inks

Dark green calligraphy ink

TECHNIQUES

Learn how to write the classic Celtic Uncial and Half-uncial scripts, first in pencil and then with a pen and ink. Practise the letter forms and check your progress against a range of the commonest mistakes before also learning how to draw decorated capital letters and even the ancient runic alphabet.

Basic Techniques

When writing Celtic scripts you are aiming to give the letters a rounded appearance and keep the weight of the letter even by holding the pen nib at a constant angle to the writing line. Try to keep lines straight and curves unbroken and even.

Preparing and loading the pen

Because the calligraphy pen has no cartridge or ink container it must be dipped in ink regularly to fill the reservoir (right). Place a nib in the end of the pen holder with firm pressure until it is secure. Attach the reservoir by sliding it onto the underside of the nib, pushing it down the nib shaft. It is important to be able to see the end of the nib a little. Do not have the reservoir too far back or too far forward.

1 To load the pen, first hold the pen in an upright position and dip about half of the nib into the ink. If you fill the nib's reservoir with too much ink it will overflow and flood the paper when you try to write.

2 Remove any excess ink by shaking the pen downwards so that the ink falls back into the ink pot. You can also wipe the nib on the side of the ink pot just to be sure.

Holding the pen

It is vital that the pen sits easily in your hand and that you never feel strained or tired while writing – the more comfortable, you are the better your calligraphy.

Hold the pen between your thumb and forefinger about 2.5cm (1in) above the nib. Take a firm grip but try to relax your hand and arm from the shoulder. Keep sitting upright with the paper straight in front of you. Ideally the paper should be placed on a board set at an angle of about 45 to 60 degrees.

For left-handed calligraphers the writing position is a little different. Find the most comfortable position by angling the paper either to the right or the left.

Drawing a pencil stave

The Celtic alphabets look best when the letters are written to a height four and a half times the width of the nib being used. Always draw up a writing stave before you begin so that your letters fit within the guide.

1 Draw a line across the paper then start measuring the distance down using a set of double pencils – the distance between the points equates to the width of a nib.

2 The distance between the lines should be 4½ pen widths so mark four spaces from the top line and then add the extra half width at the bottom.

3 Draw the bottom, or writing, line across from this mark. All your writing should be between these lines except for the ascenders and descenders – the tails of letters like 'b' and 'p'.

Placing the pen on the stave

It is easiest to start writing the Celtic scripts holding the nib at a 30 degree angle to the paper. Keep a firm grip on the pen holder but try to relax your hand and arm to the shoulder. This will help with your writing.

1 To write a straight line, like the upright of the letter 'n', place the nib against the top line at an almost flat angle then draw it straight down in a smooth movement.

2 To draw a horizontal crossing stroke turn the nib so that is at an angle of about 30°. Turn your hand from the shoulder – don't change your grip on the pen.

3 To write a curved line, like the bowl of the letter 't', return the nib to a flat angle. Make the stroke in one smooth movement to increase then decrease the width of the stroke.

Loading the pen with a brush

Sometimes you will be using tubes of gouache colour rather than calligraphy ink. This works just as well as the ink but must be applied directly to the back of the nib with a paintbrush.

Mix a little of the colour in a palette and use a size 3 brush to paint the colour onto the back of the nib so that it collects in the ink reservoir. Apply the paint carefully so that the nib does not get overloaded and do not try to fill the reservoir directly: let the paint flow down into it from the bottom of the nib.

Uncial

The Uncial alphabet is the most recognized of the Celtic scripts. It has a pleasing formation, with an open, rounded look including long strokes on some letters while others, like the D, include what is known as a fish tail. It has no capital letters as such.

DOUBLE PENCILS

Learning to write Celtic letters with double pencils shows you how they are formed and made up from a series of different strokes. Drawn large on the paper, you will be able to see your progress easily.

Bind two HB pencils together with elastic bands, pushing the points of the pencils together against a flat surface to make sure both are level. Always keep the pencils at the same flat angle to give the letters the right formation.

Writing the letter O

1 Draw a stave of 4½ pen widths using your double pencils. Start with the right-hand pencil touching the top line with the left-hand pencil at a slight angle. Draw the bowl of the letter in a smooth curve. Watch the width change as you write.

2 Take the pencils back up to the starting point and write the right-hand curve. Finish by joining up with the first curve. As you practise you will soon get the hang of joining up the different parts, creating evenly shaped letters.

Writing the letter A

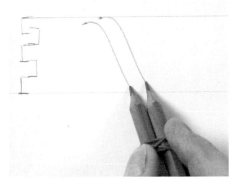

1 Even though the A includes a straight element, start with the pencils in exactly the same position as with the letter O, then bring them down to the right in a diagonal line.

2 Move halfway back up the letter and place the pencils back on the lines but this time move to the left in a slow, downward curve.

3 When the left-hand pencil reaches the writing line turn to the right sharply.

4 Move back up to join the straight line, curving upwards as you near it so that the lines of the pencils cross, creating movement in the letter.

Writing the letter F

1 More complicated letters are simply made up of the same elements. The basis of the F is a simple vertical stroke that descends below the writing line.

2 Add a decorative serif to the top with a straight diagonal movement to the left followed by a curve back to the right, finishing on the vertical lines.

3 To make the top horizontal, curve up from the end of the decoration until you hit the top writing line, letting the pencil lines cross.

4 The middle line is drawn along the bottom writing line, remembering to increase the angle of the pencils for the horizontal stroke.

5 Finish by closing up the letter with single pencil strokes across all the openings.

Writing the letter R

1 As with the F, start by writing a pair of vertical lines, finishing on the writing line.

2 Add a decoration to the top and then make a sharp rising movement to the top line.

3 Make a smooth but quick downward turn back to the verticals to form the bowl of the letter.

4 Now move down and out to the writing line, giving the leg of the letter a smooth sweep and finishing just to the right of the bowl.

Writing the letter X

1 Combining curves in a letter can be complicated. The X is especially tricky as the curves intersect. Start making the left-hand curve with the pencils on the top line.

2 Continue until you reach the writing line, moving past it and back up slightly.

3 Taking the pencils back up to the top line, sweep down in the opposite direction, completely covering the previous stroke.

4 Finish the curve as the pencil lines cross each other.

5 Return to the top and continue the curve, stopping in line with the bottom of the letter.

6 Finally, close up the gaps between the pencil lines.

WRITING IN INK

When starting to write in ink the most important factor is to keep the nib at the same angle throughout the formation of each letter. By keeping a flat angle to the paper you will form well-rounded letters whose weight, or stroke thickness, will also be correct – neither too thin nor too thick.

Some letters do require a slight change of angle when writing certain strokes. This is most common when you flatten the nib angle to write the horizontal strokes of the letters F and T. It can also stop the letters V, Y and Z looking too heavy.

Writing the letter O

1 Follow the method you used when writing with the pencils, using the ends of the nib as the two pencil points. Start with the nib point on the top line. Draw the nib round to the left, keeping the nib angle constant.

2 Place the nib back on the starting points and move to the right, finishing the letter when the nib touches the end points of the first stroke.

Writing the letter A

1 Replicate the pencil strokes with the pen and nib. Start at the top line and draw a smooth stroke with slight movements at either end to create the flicks.

2 With the nib against the first stroke begin the bowl of the letter, keeping the angle of the pen the same throughout.

3 Finish by the upright stroke. The nib angle should make the line thinnest as it approaches the end of the stroke.

Writing the letter M

1 The letter M is made up from a series of curves that, at first, can be tricky to combine. Begin with the left-hand down stroke.

2 Return to the top of the letter and finish the top curve, moving into a straight vertical stroke down to the writing line.

3 Write the final stroke in one go, making a slight curve up to the top line before moving down in a gentle curve.

NUMERALS

Numerals are relatively simple to master – yet the important skills here are scale and consistent style, so when writing letters and numbers together as part of the same project, the numbers match the style of your lettering.

Practise the numbers as below, following the arrows to see the directions of each stroke. Common mistakes (see right) will help you avoid common pitfalls with positioning and shape for both letters and numerals.

Writing the number 3

1 Write a horizontal line underneath the top writing line.

2 Move straight into the short diagonal line, keeping the nib angle the same.

3 Write the curve, sweeping down to hit the writing line into the middle of the numeral.

4 Move the nib out to the edge of the horizontal line and make a stroke back to meet the bowl of the numeral at the bottom.

Writing the number 6

1 Start writing the 6 with the same stroke as the letter O.

2 Place the nib halfway down and draw a curve to the right in a smooth stroke.

3 Returning to the top of the numeral draw a curve over the bowl to finish.

Writing the number 8

1 Write the central spine first, making an S-shaped curve between the writing lines.

2 Enclose the top loop first making a rounded bowl.

3 Balance the numeral by making the lower bowl slightly larger than the top one.

Common Mistakes

Write only 1½ pen widths above the top line and add movement to the bowl with an extra stroke

This ascender rises too high above the line

The shorter descender is more balanced

This descender drops too far below the line

Strokes do not overlap

Keep the nib at a flat angle to balance the three strokes

The two strokes cover each other

The diagonal is too thin and the horizontals too thick

Half-uncial

Sometimes called the Irish Half-uncial script, this was the style used in the great Irish manuscripts such as the Book of Kells. Developed around the eighth century, it bears many similarities to the slightly earlier Uncial alphabet, with its open, rounded forms. It is pleasing to the eye, and its simplicity makes it easily read.

PRACTISING WITH DOUBLE PENCILS

Although the Half-uncial alphabet has many similarities to the Uncial script it is important to practise writing the letters with pencils first to become familiar with the different letter forms.

Writing the letter A

1 Begin making a wide, sweeping curve stroke with the double pencils. When the bottom pencil hits the writing line move back up and stop.

2 Finish the curve at the top by bringing the lines across to the right and down so that they end up in line with the bottom stroke.

3 Start the vertical stroke just to the right of the previous stroke and bring it back towards the bowl of the letter before going straight down. Finish with a pronounced curve, and close up the gap with a single stroke.

Writing the letter N

1 The Half-uncial N is very different from the modern letter. Start with a vertical line that descends below the writing line.

2 Add decoration to the top of the letter and make a slightly curved diagonal down to the writing line.

3 Draw a straight vertical to meet the end points of the diagonal line.

4 Add some decoration to the top of the second vertical and finish by closing up the bottoms of both vertical strokes.

Writing the letter Y

1 The key to writing letters with diagonal strokes is to balance the various parts that make it up. Start the Y with a straight diagonal between the two writing lines.

2 Start the second stroke with a quick curve but then bring it down to meet the end points of the existing stroke, ensuring the two sides balance.

3 Continue the stroke below the line but quickly turn it into a smooth curve that heads back up towards the writing line.

4 Finish by enclosing the bottom of the letter.

WRITING IN INK

To give the right weight to the pen-made strokes Half-uncial letters need to be written at a flat angle. They should be rounded in appearance, even when they include straight elements, as with the letter N, where the first downward stroke goes below the writing line. If you find the spacing between words is too long, or your writing has finished too short at the end of a line, then it is possible to add length to some of the finished strokes, as in the letter E. This could be a Celtic knot, scroll or triskele design added to the tip to fill the space.

Writing the letter L

1 Begin the ascender above the top line and write the letter in one stroke, giving it a strong, fluid, curved appearance.

2 Finish the letter by adding a small decorative flourish to the top of the ascender.

Writing the letter X

1 The letter X is composed of a series of rounded elements, the first of which is a tall anticlockwise curve between the writing lines of the stave.

2 Add a return to the bottom of the curve, meeting the first line on the writing line.

3 The third stroke is a mirror image of the first. Make sure the widest part of the curve covers the same part of the first stroke.

4 Finish by completing the curve at the top of the right-hand element of the letter.

Writing the letter B

1 The main structure of the letter B replicates the L: give the form a smooth, flowing line.

2 Create the round bowl of the letter using all the space between the lines.

3 Emphasize the fish tail by adding a decorative stroke to the top of the vertical.

Writing the letter F

1 Start with the vertical, dropping it below the writing line as with the letter N.

2 Make the loop of the F starting with the thinnest part of the nib.

3 Finish with a straight horizontal stroke along the writing line.

Common Mistakes

The horizontal stroke is too thin

The correct nib angle makes the top of the letter a suitable width

The different elements of the M are too widely spaced

Keep the gaps in the letter even

Ensure the descender only drops 1½ pen widths below the writing line

The curved elements of the letter are too upright

Curves give the Half-uncial letters their flowing form

The descender is too long

Square Capitals

Celtic manuscripts used drawn letters as well as the Uncial and Half-uncial scripts. First outlined then filled in with ink, the letters were placed very close to each other. They were often decorated with bright coloured panels as well as Celtic knots.

DRAWING SQUARE CAPITALS

Drawn between two pencil lines roughly 4cm (1½in) apart, the letters are first worked lightly with a soft pencil, then drawn over with a fine line black pen. Celtic knotwork panels make up some of the letters – the R is a good example showing the interlacing knotwork in the centre bar of the letter. When used in manuscript the letters of this alphabet are usually surrounded by a band of straight coloured lines at the top and bottom of the drawn line of text, and the height of each letter is usually written inside these painted lines.

Writing the letter D

1 Draw the outer lines of the vertical element first, giving them both slight inward curves.

2 Draw the curves of the right-hand part of the letter, giving the letter an even thickness.

3 Draw the decoration inside the letter, adding dots to finish, then go over the whole letter with a fine line black pen.

Writing the letter R

1 Start the letter like the D with concave vertical strokes, then add a smooth bowl curving towards the centre of the vertical.

2 Bring the bowl to a point to the right of the vertical and start designing the knotwork by drawing the shape with a single line.

3 Bring the knotwork twice around the vertical, remembering to make the design move over and under itself in turn.

4 Add in the foot of the letter, widening it to match the bottom of the vertical but not going out wider than the bowl.

5 Go over the knotwork to make it up from two lines of pencil work.

6 Cover all the pencil with ink from a fine line black pen.

Common Mistakes

Do not draw the letters too wide – they should always be rectangular in shape, narrow and drawn close together on the writing line.

Do not draw the descender stroke too far below the writing line and check where the elements of the letter join each other.

Do not make the central element too long. Make the strokes shorter and less pronounced.

Cursive Capitals

This alphabet is based on letters found in the Lindisfarne Gospels. Also drawn and filled in with ink, some of the letters and spacing were painted in colour. Both colour and pattern played important roles with Celtic knot designs filling any open spaces.

DRAWING CURSIVE CAPITALS

Cursive capitals are more rounded than the square capitals and some letters use decorations like zoomorphic animal heads to finish off the end of a letter. Other differences include some letters, such as the L, rising slightly above the top line while parts of the letters X and Y fall below the writing line.

Writing the letter S

1 Begin with a smooth curve from the top to the writing line. Add the second side of the letter, smoothly following the rhythm of the first line but narrowing at top and bottom.

2 Add the tail to the base, opening it out and enclosing with a short curved line.

3 Repeat at the top of the letter, making the curves slightly smaller to give the letter balance. Cover the pencil with black ink and rub out any remaining pencil marks.

Writing the letter M

1 Using a soft pencil, draw a very gently curved vertical line from the top line down to the writing line.

2 Draw in the other side of the vertical, starting just below the top line to allow for the curve to follow.

3 The left-hand curve of the letter is narrower than might be expected. Widen the foot at the bottom.

4 The right-hand curve is slightly wider to ensure the three feet are evenly spaced.

5 Enclose the feet and top of the vertical then add decoration inside the letter.

6 Cover the whole letter in black ink from a fine line pen.

Common Mistakes

Try not to make the curved letters too round in appearance; the letter O especially should be oval in shape. Always draw the letters between the top and bottom lines.

Draw the letters with even spaces between each letter and with extra space between each word.

Avoid drawing ascenders and descenders too long above and below the lines. Draw them no more than 1cm (½in) below or above the line.

Runic Characters

The runic letters originate from Scandinavia and are much older than the Celtic alphabets. The characters are different to other alphabets in as much as they are symbols that do not correspond to specific letters of the modern alphabet. Originally carved on bone, wood and stone, they are often seen on standing stones or archaeological finds such as carved hair combs. Runes were used for divination, and an object marked with one of the symbols was sometimes carried by the owner as a talisman for good luck or a safe journey.

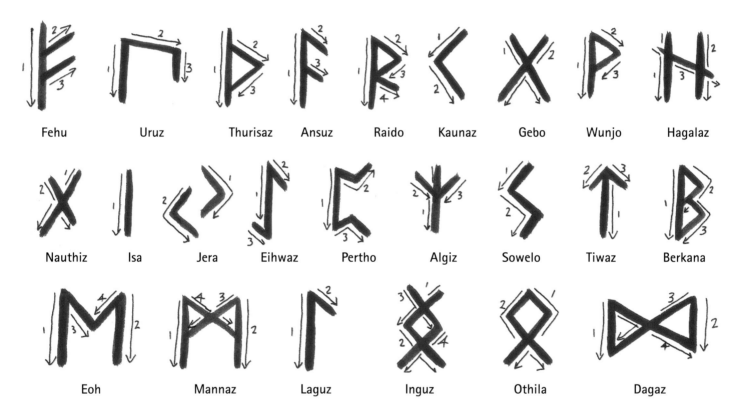

Fehu   Uruz   Thurisaz   Ansuz   Raido   Kaunaz   Gebo   Wunjo   Hagalaz

Nauthiz   Isa   Jera   Eihwaz   Pertho   Algiz   Sowelo   Tiwaz   Berkana

Eoh   Mannaz   Laguz   Inguz   Othila   Dagaz

WRITING RUNIC CHARACTERS

As all of the runic characters are made up of a series of free-flowing lines they do not suit being written with a steel-nibbed calligraphy pen which will not be able to replicate the even width of the elements. Instead it is best to write the characters using a soft, pointed paintbrush – ideally made of sable in size 1 or 2.

Start at the top of the stroke and write each character freehand. You do not draw lines before painting these symbols but it may help you to use writing lines when practising them on paper. A felt tip pen is also useful for practice in drawing the lines of the runes, as the felt tip pen flows easily over the surface.

Writing the character Raido

1 Start with a simple vertical line between the writing lines.

2 Draw a triangular shape, rejoining the centre line halfway along its length.

3 The final line should be written at the same angle as the top diagonal but it should stop well short of the bottom writing line.

Writing the character Eihwaz

1 Many runic characters are based around a straight vertical line. Start the Eihwaz with one.

2 The simple diagonals should be very short and run parallel to each other.

Writing the character Inguz

1 Some runic characters do look complicated but are generally very simple to write. Start the Inguz with a pair of diagonals at right angles to each other.

2 Repeat the diagonals in the opposite direction to create the finished character. Ensure that the two sides balance each other.

Writing the character Dagaz

1 The size of the characters on the page can vary in the Runic alphabet. Start the Dagaz with a vertical and a wide diagonal from the top of the line.

2 Draw a second vertical line to create a form like a very wide capital letter N.

3 Finish the character by adding a second diagonal that mirrors the first.

Common Mistakes

Try to keep the paint or ink flowing freely and write each rune symbol with confidence. It does not matter if they are not of equal size – some of the symbols are smaller and others larger. Try to keep the brushstrokes all the same thickness – it will help make the runes look even, whatever their size on the page.

37

PROJECTS

Now that you've mastered the basic Celtic alphabets, put your hard work into practice
in a range of beautiful projects that will show off your skills as well as enhancing your
home and making beautiful gifts for your family and friends.

Wishing Stone

You can turn a stone found on any beach into a wishing stone, by holding it in your hand and feeling the ancient stone as you make a wish. Write in a freehand Uncial script with a steel pen using gouache colour to give an authentic look, then varnish the stone with a spirit varnish to seal the design.

Materials

Flat beach stone

Gouache colour – red, blue, cream, purple, green and white

Palette

Gum arabic

Size 1½ nib

Reservoir

Pen holder

Water jar

HB pencil

Size 5 and 1 brushes

Satin wood, spirit-based varnish

Flat varnishing brush

1 Wash the stone, allowing it to dry completely. Mix the purple gouache in a palette with a drop of gum arabic and water to the consistency of single cream with the size 5 brush. Place the size 1½ nib into the holder and push the reservoir into the nib. Now brush the mixed gouache onto the back of the nib.

2 Using the pen write the words *cloch mianach*, meaning 'wishing stone', freestyle – without pencil lines – in Uncial script. You could practise the words on paper first to become confident with the writing.

3 When the lettering is dry, lightly pencil the Celtic knot design (page 117) onto the centre of the stone. Now use the size 1 brush loaded with the mixed gouache and go over the pencil lines until none show, and paint in the Celtic knot.

4 When the gouache is completely dry, apply the varnish sparingly over the lettering with the flat brush. Allow to dry overnight before handling the stone.

Name Plaque on Wood

This name plaque makes an unusual gift for a child or adult to adorn a bedroom door or wall. It is written on wood, a material sacred to the Celts, in the Uncial script with the use of interlacing Celtic designs above and below the name.

1 Varnish the wooden plaque using a flat varnish brush, stroking the varnish on as evenly as possible. The varnish will lift the grain so allow it to dry for 24 hours then work the fine sandpaper in a slow, even motion along the grain of the wood, taking off the excess dust with a soft cloth.

2 Copy the plaque's boundaries onto some tracing paper by drawing round it with a 2B pencil.

Materials

Oval wood plaque

Satin wood, spirit-based varnish

Flat varnish brush

Fine sandpaper

Soft cloth

Tracing paper

H and 2B pencils

Ruler

Eraser

Size 0 nib

Reservoir

Pen holder

Fine line black pen

Masking tape

3 Measure the width of the plaque to discover the length of available writing space and draw a stave onto a piece of practice paper.

4 Using a size 0 nib draw up a stave of 4½ pen widths of the length measured in the previous step on a piece of plain paper, adding two pen widths above and below for the initial cap and marking the available length. Using the same nib, start practising writing your name. If it is too long or short try again using a smaller or bigger nib, always discovering the height of the lettering by creating a stave using 4½ pen widths.

5 Trace the knot designs top and bottom from the template (page 122) onto the top and bottom of the trace making sure they are centred. Now trace over the name with a soft pencil.

6 Go over the pencil lines with a fine pen so that you don't lose the definition of the lines when you carbonize the back of the paper.

7 Use the 2B pencil to carbonize the back of the tracing paper then place the trace onto the plaque and stick down on all four sides with masking tape. Go over all the black lines with the hard pencil to transfer the design from the underside tracing to the wooden plaque. Lift one corner of the tracing paper to make sure the design is showing.

8 Take the fine line black pen and draw over all the pencil lines on the surface of the plaque. Move the plaque so that your hand stays in roughly the same position as you work.

9 Fill in the black areas of the letters and add the dots and decorations. Take care not to smudge the ink: only work in one direction so that your hand is never over the lettering. Leave to dry completely for a few hours.

10 Now seal the design by using a wide brush to cover the surface with varnish. Allow to dry for a day before handling.

Gaelic House-Blessing Card

It was traditional in the Celtic lands to give a blessing for a new home. This Gaelic blessing would be an ideal greetings card for a friend moving into a new house. It is written in the Irish Half-uncial script, using Celtic interlacing corner designs, and is finished with random colour panels in the text.

2 Fold a sheet of A4 paper in half to make an A5 card. Draw four lines 1cm (½in) in from the edge around the card with a soft pencil then find the centre point and draw a line down the card.

3 Trace the knot design from the template (page 117) in pencil then go over it in pen so that it retains definition when carbonized.

1 Using the size 2 nib for the initial cap and the size 3 for the rest of the lettering, draw 4½ pen-width staves onto a piece of cartridge paper and practise the Half-uncial script.

Materials

Size 2 and 3 nibs	Ruler
Pen holder	Size 5 and 1 brushes
2 reservoirs	Gouache colour – green,
Black calligraphy ink	gold, red, blue and yellow
White cartridge paper	Gum arabic
Tracing paper	Palette
H and 2B pencils	Water jar
Fine line black pen	Eraser
A4 sheet of card	A5 size envelope

4 Carbonize the back, then cut out the motif and place it in the corner of the card sticking it down with masking tape.

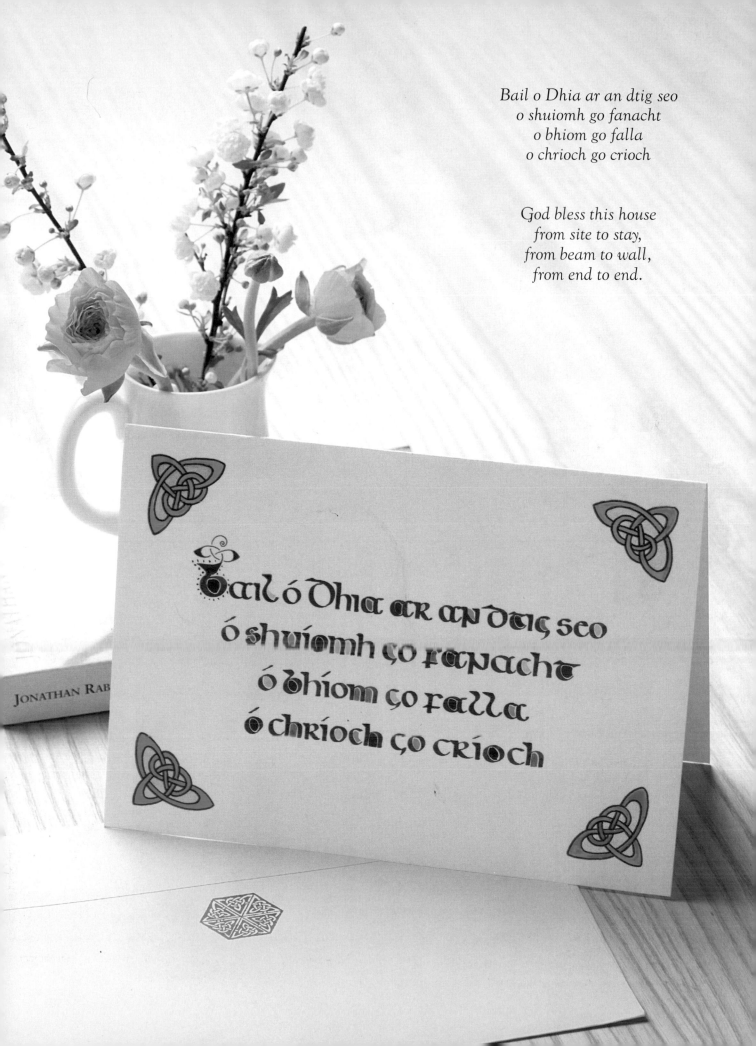

Bail o Dhia ar an dtig seo
o shuiomh go fanacht
o bhiom go falla
o chrioch go crioch

God bless this house
from site to stay,
from beam to wall,
from end to end.

5 Use the hard pencil to transfer the design through to the card. Move the motif to all the corners of the card and repeat.

6 Measure 5cm (2in) from the top of the card and draw a line across the card with the soft pencil to make the top of the upper stave. Now draw the other lines to make staves for the four lines of text. Allow 1cm (½in) between the lines, making sure you allow for the larger initial letter at the beginning of the first line.

7 Measure the length of the practice lines and mark them onto the final sheet, centred around the vertical line. Write the Celtic blessing in black ink, starting with the initial letter B in the size 2 nib followed by the rest of the text in a size 3 nib. Add decorative space fillers at the end of each line if necessary.

8 Paint the knot decorations with a fine, size 5 brush using green gouache mixed with a drop of gum arabic, then fill in the rest of the design with gold.

9 When dry, use the fine line pen to outline the corner designs in an over and under pattern.

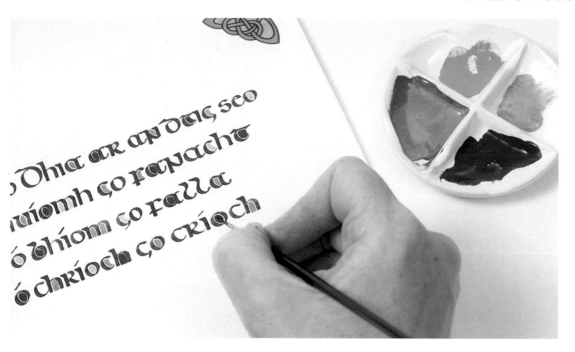

10 Mix up a little of the other coloured gouache and using the size 1 brush, decorate some of the letters at random.

11 To finish the card, add dots around the initial cap with the size 0 brush to illuminate it.

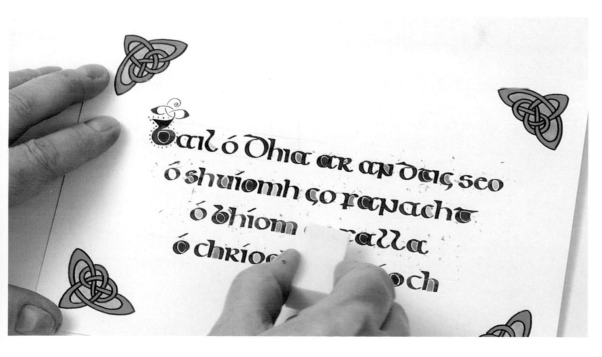

12 Once the paint is completely dry carefully rub out the pencil lines with a soft eraser.

Wooden Picture Frame

Here, a simple wooden frame is painted in a pastel colour using water-based craft paint.

A black Celtic knot border has been added around all four sides, and each corner has a

simple Celtic square motif painted with lavender pearlized paint.

1 Cover the plain wooden frame with the pastel acrylic paint using a flat brush to stroke on the paint evenly, allowing it to dry completely. Trace the Celtic knot border design from the template (page 117). Use the soft pencil to carbonize the back of the design before tracing the Celtic design onto each edge of the frame with a hard pencil.

2 Use the fine line black pen to go over the pencil lines on each side of the frame.

Materials

Wooden picture frame

Acrylic pastel green paint

Flat soft brush

Tracing paper

Masking tape

H and 2B pencils

Fine line black pen

Metallic acrylic paint

Size 0 brush

3 Trace the corner design (page 117) onto all 4 corners of the frame. Work in the same way as before, carbonizing the pattern before transferring the design onto the frame using the hard pencil and covering with the fine line black pen.

4 Emphasize the pointed corners of the knot design on both the corner motifs and border by thickening the insides of the turns with the black pen.

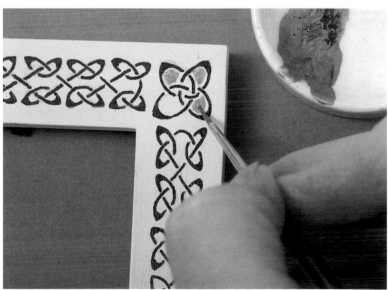

5 Highlight the corner designs by filling in the motifs with the metallic acrylic paint, using a size 0 brush.

Scottish Travel Blessing

The ancient people of Celtic lands often used travel blessings. This blessing comes from the Isle of Skye, on the west coast of Scotland, which still holds to age-old Celtic traditions. Written in Gaelic, this blessing wishes the safe return of a loved one travelling far away from home. The translation can be found overleaf.

Materials

A3 tracing paper
Stencil card (24cm/ 9½in square)
H and 2B pencils
Cutting board
Craft knife
Masking tape
A3 green Canson card
Gold pearlescent ink
Palette
Stippling brush
Water jar
A3 cartridge paper
Pen holder
Size 0 and 1½ nibs
2 reservoirs
Black calligraphy ink
30cm (12in) ruler
Zinc white gouache
Gum arabic
Size 3 brush for mixing
Windsor green gouache
Eraser

1 Trace the Celtic star motif from the template (page 123). Take the stencil card and find the centre point by measuring the card both ways and draw two lines to make a cross in the centre. Now carbonize the reverse of the tracing paper with the 2B pencil before placing it onto the middle of the stencil card. With an H pencil go over the design, transferring it to the card.

2 Place the stencil card on a cutting board and carefully cut out the design with a craft knife. Take care not to accidentally cut between the line design.

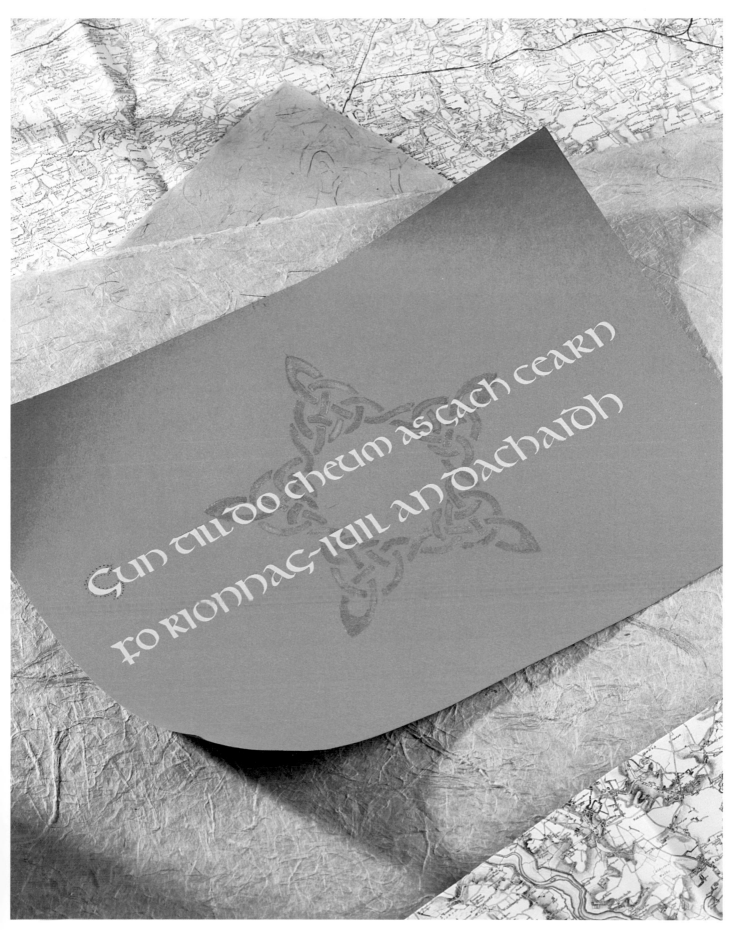

Gun till do cheum as gach cearn
fo rionnag-iuil an dachaidh

3 Measure the A3 green card to find the middle points of each side and mark lines 10cm (4in) in from the edges. Place the stencil onto the green card so that the lines match up and and stick in place with masking tape.

4 Now mix some gold ink into a palette and dip in the stippling brush, taking off the excess ink on a spare piece of card, by pressing and using circular movements. Then stipple through the cut stencil to apply the gold colour. Try not to put too much paint onto the stencil as it can seep under the cut stencil and spoil the design.

Tip

● When cutting the stencil take care to leave small joins of paper where one part of the design goes underneath another. If you cut too close you may not be able to make out which part of the design is uppermost.

● The stencil card can be tough to cut through. If the blade doesn't go all the way through turn the card over and press gently along the impression of the cut that will be showing through to make the final cut.

⁝ Ꝼun till do cheum as ꞇach cearn

⁝ ꝼo rionnaꞇ-iuil an dachai

5 Practise the writing on a piece of A3 cartridge paper. Draw a stave with the size 0 nib by drawing lines top and bottom to give the x height – this is for the letter G. Now do the same for the rest of the writing using a size 1½ nib. Measure the lines of writing.

6 Transfer the writing lines to the green card. Start by measuring down from the top of the green card 10cm (4in). Draw a pencil line lightly with a soft pencil for the top line of the writing. Leave 3cm (1¼in) between the writing lines. Measure the practice writing and draw a start point onto the green card.

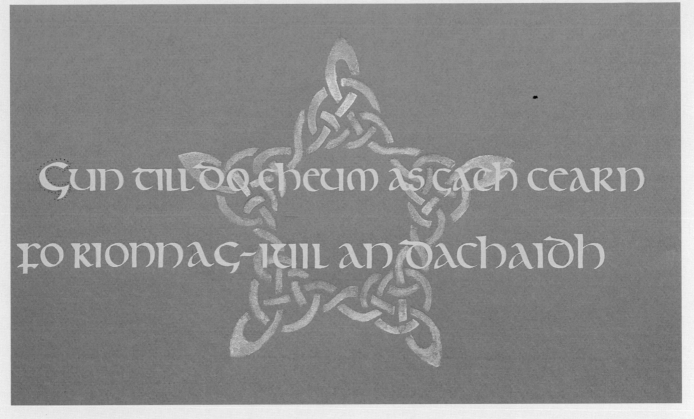

Gun till do cheum as gach cearn

Fo rionnag-iuil an dachaidh

May your steps return from all the corners of

the globe under the guidance of the star that

points to home.

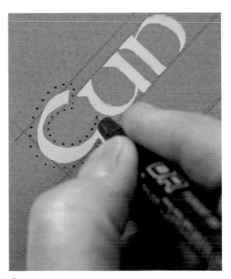

7 Mix the white gouache with a drop of gum arabic and a little water, adding a little drop of green gouache to the palette and mixing well using the size 3 brush to make a very pale green that will be visible against the dark green. Write the card, starting with the size 0 nib for the letter G and continuing with the size 1½ nib for the two lines of writing.

8 When the writing is completely dry, add black dots around the letter. Rub all the pencil lines out when completely dry.

Illuminated Letter R

Manuscript illumination was regarded as one of the most beautiful and skilled

techniques of the scribe. Here, you can make your own illuminated letter to frame.

Draw an initial letter and adapt the Celtic knot pattern from the template on

page 119, adding an angel or animal design to complete the project.

1 Trace the letter and angel from the template (page 119) and carbonize the back before placing it on the white parchment card and transferring the design onto the card with a hard pencil.

Materials

Tracing paper

H and 2B pencils

White parchment card

Fine line black pen

Gouache colour – yellow, purple, red, white and gold

Gum arabic

Palette

Water jar

Size 0, 1, 2 and 4 brushes

2 Start by drawing over the pencil lines with the fine line black pen, making it easier to paint the yellow inside the fine Celtic knotwork.

3 Mix some yellow gouache with a drop of gum arabic and a little water in a palette. Use the size 1 brush to start painting in the yellow edging. Next, mix some purple with a drop of white in the same way, using the size 3 brush in the larger areas. Paint an outline along the black edge first then fill in the rest of the area.

4 Now start painting the angel using the gold gouache: mix in the same way and paint in the wings, halo and trumpet. Cover the whole wing including the black lines.

5 Paint in the rest of the angel using red, orange and pink gouache, mixed from the colours on the palette.

6 Now mix some more white into the purple gouache to make a lilac colour. Paint a fine line with the size 1 brush, next to the black outline on the outside edge of the purple.

Tip

When creating a complex design it can be easier to draw the outline before painting so that the area for each colour is well differentiated.

7 Go over the black outlines of the wings and any other part that has been accidentally covered with paint using the fine line black pen.

8 Finally, mix red gouache, gum arabic and water and use the size 0 brush to put dots all the way around the letter and angel.

Ex Libris Book Plate

This gospel-inspired book plate uses curved capital letters taken from the Lindisfarne

Gospels written on Holy Island, Northumberland. The space in the centre of the design

is left blank so that the owner's name can be added.

Materials

Practice paper
30cm (12in) ruler
H and 2B pencils
A4 tracing paper
Masking tape
Fine line black pen
Size 000, 0 and 4
    brushes
Gouache colour –
    crimson, scarlet, blue,
    green, yellow and white
A4 lilac card
Black calligraphy ink
Gum arabic
Palette
Water jar
Silk marbled paper
PVA glue
Eraser

1 Draw up a grid on a practice sheet of card 11.5cm (4½in) wide and 15cm (6in) high, making spaces for two lines of letters 4cm (1½in) high and the different knotwork decorations.

2 Trace the letters from the template alphabet and transfer them to the practice paper, placing the top line slightly to the left of centre to allow for a piece of knotwork decoration.

3 Trace in the knotwork panels then work up the colours, experimenting with different colour combinations. Use gouache paints and a size 0 brush.

4 Take the final card and replicate the box then trace in the letters and knotwork again. Then cover the pencil lines with the fine line black pen.

5 Fill in the letters with black calligraphy ink using a size 0 brush.

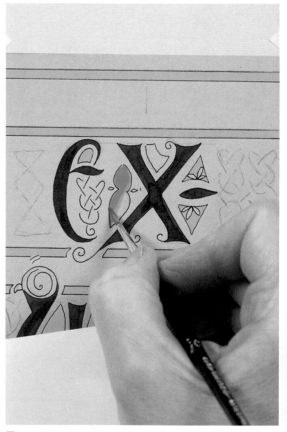

6 Cover the lines of the box and the letter decorations using a fine line black pen.

7 Paint in the colour panels following the practice sheet you made earlier.

8 Trace the knotwork used at the top and bottom from the template (page 120) and transfer them onto the card, then go over the pencil lines using the fine line black pen.

9 Highlight the rest of the decoration with dots, using red gouache and a size 000 brush.

10 Stick the card to a piece of silk marbled paper with PVA glue then rub out any remaining pencil lines with an eraser.

Uncial Place Card

This place card project is easy to achieve and is perfect for a special occasion, such as a

dinner party or wedding. The Uncial script is complemented with an imaginative

romantic heart motif and a simple Celtic border design.

1 Measure across the front of the place card to find the centre, draw a line down the centre, leaving space for the main heart motif. Trace the heart and knotwork border design from the template (page 117) and carbonize the back before placing it over the centre line and tracing through with a hard pencil.

2 Draw a stave 4½ pen widths high on a spare card to find the height of the Uncial lettering and rule across in pencil before practising writing the name.

Materials

30cm (12in) ruler
White card cut to A5 size
   or bought place card
Tracing paper
H and 2B pencils
Masking tape
Pen holder
Size 3 nib and reservoir
Black calligraphy ink
Size 0 brush
Red gouache
Palette
Gum arabic
Water jar
Fine line black pen
Ink drawing pen
Eraser

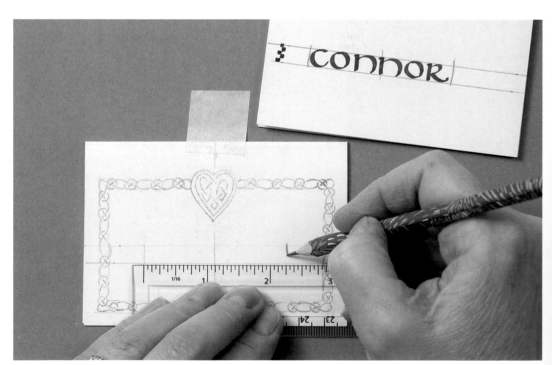

3 Now measure the length of the word and mark the start and finish on the place card, centring it on the pencil line drawn in Step 1.

4 Paint in the heart with red gouache, after mixing a little in the palette with a drop of gum arabic and water. Use the size 0 sable brush and leave to dry. Write the name in black ink with the size 3 nib.

5 Go over the design inside the heart with a permanent fine line black pen and then add dots around the heart. Finally use an ink drawing pen to go over the border. When dry rub out the pencil lines.

Ceilidh Invitation

For many centuries in Celtic lands, traditional music and dancing have been enjoyed and are still practised today. This card design includes traditional instruments, and the Celtic corner border with flowers and motifs is inspired by the Book of Kells.

Materials

Practice paper

Compass

Pen holder

Light blue silk paper

Size 2½ nib and reservoir

Black calligraphy ink

30cm (12in) ruler

Tracing paper

H and 2B pencils

Masking tape

Fine line black pen

Automatic 5-point pen

Size 000, 1 and 4
    brushes

Gouache colour – scarlet,
    Prussian blue, emerald
    green, lemon yellow and
    zinc white

Gum arabic

Palette

Water jar

Eraser

Blue A4 card

1 Draw a 5cm (2in) diameter circle with a compass on a sheet of practice paper then draw a stave inside with a pen and size 2½ nib. Recalibrate the compass and draw the bottom writing line from the end of the stave.

2 Practise writing the word 'ceilidh' in Half-uncial letters, curving it in both directions.

3 Find the centre of the card by drawing lines from the middle of both sides then draw a cross on a piece of tracing paper and trace the central design. Carbonize the back and transfer it to the silk paper, centring it over the cross.

4 Cover the pencil design with fine line black pen.

5 Draw a pencil rectangle around the edge, then place a tracing of the corner motif template (page 121) on each corner and transfer, covering with ink.

6 Pencil in the writing circles onto the paper with the compass and write in the letters with ink.

7 Draw in the curved musical staves with a five-pronged automatic pen.

8 Draw musical notes onto the staves using the fine line black pen then colour in the decoration with gouache and a fine paintbrush.

Tip

When writing in a circle with a pen and nib turn the paper as you move from letter to letter so that your pen is always upright.

9 Trace musical instruments (page 120) and transfer them onto the centre of the invitation. Draw over with the black pen. Stick the paper onto a sheet of stiff card.

Slate Welcome Sign

This bright bold sign, reading 'Failte', means 'welcome' in Gaelic. Painted on slate, a

natural ancient surface, in angular square capitals in the style of the great manuscript

books of the eighth century, this sign could have come from early Celtic times.

1 Use the image below as a template and enlarge it on a photocopier, then transfer the design to a sheet of tracing paper. Keep the lines of each letter as straight as possible. Draw the decoration around the wording (page 124).

Materials

A4 tracing paper
White chalk
Piece of slate
30cm (12in) ruler
White chinagraph pencil
Masking tape
Ballpoint pen
Acrylic colours – red, blue,
   green, yellow and white
Size 1 brush
Size 3 brush for mixing
Palette
Water jar
Fine line black pen
Soft rag

2 Carbonize the back of the tracing paper with white chalk, making sure you have a lot of chalk on the tracing otherwise the design will not transfer successfully to the slate.

Create a colour sketch of your design before starting to work on the slate to check that the colours you have chosen combine together well.

3 Take the slate and find the centre point by measuring it across and down, marking at top and bottom with a white chinagraph pencil. Draw a line from top to bottom and side to side. Place the trace in the centre of the slate, sticking it in place with masking tape. Now use the ballpoint pen to draw along your pencil lines with firm pressure to transfer the design onto the slate.

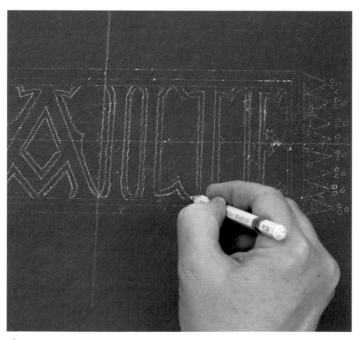

4 Before you start painting use the chinagraph pencil to emphasize the traced image.

5 Paint the lettering of the word 'failte' using the size 1 brush and red acrylic paint. Mix a little paint into a palette with the size 3 brush and add enough water to make it a smooth consistency. Do not mix too much water and make the paint too runny.

6 When the red paint is dry continue to paint with the yellow, blue and green paints. Allow each to dry before applying the next colour. You will need to paint all the colours several times to achieve a solid, consistent finish on the dark slate.

7 Now use the permanent marker pen to highlight the edges of each colour and to add some Celtic knots to the design. Either draw your own designs freehand or trace one of the templates (pages 116–125) in the same way as before.

8 Finish the design by using a soft rag and some water to remove any white chinagraph or chalk lines still visible on the slate.

Anniversary Plaque

Here is a unique project to give as an Anniversary gift to remember a special day. Based

on the pages of illumination from the Book of Kells, it uses a border of interlacing

Celtic knots of bright colours to add a textured look to the project.

1 Take A3 tracing paper and draw a line across for the top of the frame. Trace the three border elements from the templates (page 124) onto a small sheet of tracing paper and place this underneath the A3 tracing paper and first trace a corner section. Then move the traced template so that a rectangular element is abutting the corner and trace this. Continue until the entire frame is on the large piece of tracing paper.

2 On a sheet of A3 card make a mark 7.5cm (3in) up then a full line 2cm (¾in) above. Measure across the page and mark the centre point and draw a vertical line. Measure 10cm (4in) above the top line and make another mark.

Materials

A3 and A4 tracing paper
46/60cm (18/24in) ruler
Flexible curve
H and 2B pencils
Fine line black pen
Cream A3 card
Practice paper
Pen holder
Size 0 nib and reservoir
Black calligraphy ink
Colour pencils – cerise,
    purple, green and yellow

3 Take a flexible curve and bend it into an even curve. Place its centre on the mark just made and draw a curve. Measure up 2cm (¾in) and draw a second curve, slightly widening the arc of the flexible curve to maintain the ratio between the lines.

4 Trace the heart motif from the template (page 125) and carbonize the back before placing it on the centre line 2cm (¾in) above the horizontal line, transferring the design to the card.

5 Very lightly plot the letters freehand in pencil between the curves, spacing them so that the first and last letters match horizontally.

6 Trace the caps from the template (page 125) or draw your own onto a sheet of tracing paper then centre the cap across the writing lines at the left-hand extremity of the curves and transfer the design.

Tip

● When using a combination of templates take care to position each one correctly.

● To give your flexible curve an even curve, bend it around a dinner plate, stool seat, table edge or any other large rounded object.

7 Write the letters of the names onto the card, using the pencil marks as a guide.

8 Take the fine line black pen and go over the pencil cap letters and draw the outlines of the decoration inside the letters.

9 Draw horizontal writing lines on a practice sheet and write the date, then measure the length.

10 Transfer the length to the card, centring it on the vertical line then begin writing in the date in ink.

11 Use colour pencils to add colour to the capped letters and the letter decoration.

12 Take the traced frame, carbonize the back and transfer the design onto the card, centring it around the design. Allow space above the names to add in zoomorphic decoration.

13 Go over the pencil with the fine line black pen.

14 Add colour to the knotwork, starting with light purple and continuing in dark purple, green and yellow.

15 Trace the zoomorphic animals (page 125) and transfer them to the main sheet. Finish by adding decoration around the date and colour to the heart and animals.

Celtic Bookmark

With this Celtic astronomical blessing of the Sun, Moon and stars, this bookmark will always be useful to keep your place in your favourite book. It is written in Irish Gaelic and topped with a Celtic cross motive, which in Celtic Christian times represented great spirituality and protection.

1 Cut a rectangular bookmark from the sheet of watercolour card then draw a border 3mm (¹/₈in) around the edge with a fine line black pen, leaving 1cm (½in) from the top of the card to allow for the ribbon hole.

Materials

Craft knife or scissors
Cutting board
Watercolour card
Fine line black pen
2B and H pencils
Tracing paper
Size 0 brush
Pearlized turquoise ink
Palette
Red and dark green
    waterproof ink
Water jar
Gum arabic
Cartridge paper
Size 3 brush for mixing
Size 5 nib and reservoir
Pen holder
Hole punch
Tartan ribbon (30cm/12in)

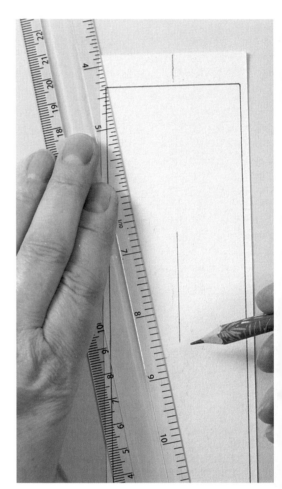

2 To position the Celtic cross centrally, measure the width of the card and mark the middle with a pencil. Draw a line, allowing space for the Celtic cross and then continue marking a pencil line in the middle.

3 Trace the design from the template (page 122) or design your own Celtic cross. Carbonize the tracing and transfer to the card with a sharp, hard pencil.

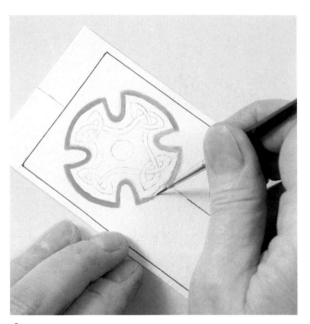

4 Use the size 0 brush with the turquoise pearlized ink, to paint the outside edge of the design.

5 Continue by adding the dark green ink into the background of the design, then finish by filling in the knotwork with red ink.

꞊ Ꝺeꞑꞑꞑꞑꞑcꞑ Ꝺoᵯ, ꞑ Ꝺꞑiꞑ, ꞑꞑ cꞑeꞑꞑꞑcꞑ ꞑꞑꞑ os ᵯo cꞑeꞑꞑꞑ

꞊ Ꝺeꞑꞑꞑꞑcꞑ Ꝺoᵯ, ꞑꝺꞑiꞑ, ꞑꞑ ꞑꞑꞑ

6 Rule a sheet of cartridge paper with two staves using the size 5 nib and write out the verse. At this stage just practise forming the letters, do not worry about fitting the words onto the bookmark.

7 Cut out the calligraphy from the practice sheet and lay it on a spare bookmark to discover the ideal position and length of each line.

8 Rule up staves on the bookmark and measure the length of each practice line. Centre each measurement, marking the start of each line of text.

9 Write the blessing onto the bookmark using the same nib as the practice sheet.

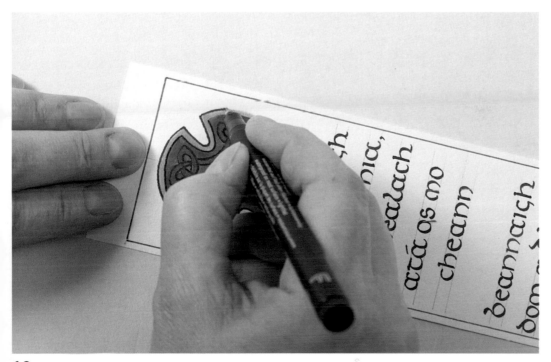

10 Use the fine line black pen and go over all the lines, adding some dots around the cross then, when everything is dry, rub out the pencil lines, and punch a hole through the top of the bookmark, adding the tartan coloured ribbon.

Deannaigh dom, a Dhia, an ghealach ata os mo cheann.

Deannaigh dom, a Dhia, an talamh ata fum.

Bless to me, O God, the moon that is above me.

Bless to me, O God, the earth that is beneath me.

Chinese Proverb

All Chinese proverbs have an ancient wisdom at their heart, and this is no exception:

'Rather light a candle, than complain about the dark'. This project uses a silver candle-

shaped design of an interlacing Celtic knotwork panel, whilst the first line of the

proverb is written in an arc and depicts the glow from the candle flame.

Materials

Compass
H and 2B pencils
A3 dark blue paper
Gold and silver metallic
    fibre pens
A4 tracing paper
Pen holder
Size 2½ nib and reservoir
Silver and gold metallic
    ink
Size 0 brush

1 On a practice sheet draw a centre line down then mark 9cm (3½in) down and draw a horizontal crossing line. Set the compass to 5cm (2in) and place on the crossing point. This is the writing line. Draw a stave out from this line using a size 2½ nib then recalibrate the compass on the outer edge of the stave to make the upper writing line.

2 Draw a horizontal line 2.5cm (1in) either side of the mark made in the previous step to form the top of the candle and three vertical lines 1.25cm (½in), 1.5cm (¾in) and 2.5cm (1in) from the centre to form the sides of the candle and two writing columns. Mark the columns with 6mm (¼in) spaces for the letters divided by 4mm (⅛in) gaps with 8mm (⅝in) gaps between the words on the left-hand column and 10mm (¾in) gaps between the words on the right-hand column, leaving space at the bottom for a knotwork decoration.

3 Practise writing the Uncial lettering around the circular stave. Very lightly pencil in the lettering and draw a horizontal line to confirm the start and end are level then rewrite in ink using the size 2½ nib.

ba chóir coinneal a lasadh is cana
bheith ag gearán faoin dorcadas

4 Replicate the pencil lines on a piece of card and draw round the candle with a thick-ended gold fibre pen.

5 Transfer a tracing of the knotwork decoration (page 120) into the centre of the candle and cover with a fine point silver metallic pen.

Tip

● Keep metallic ink well-stirred to stop it separating with the water rising to the top. Use a fine brush to place the ink onto the nib.

● After using metallic ink be very careful when erasing pencil lines as the ink smudges easily.

6 Write the circular lettering using metallic gold ink.

7 Draw the outline of the flame in pencil then fill in with gold ink using a fine size 0 paintbrush.

8 Write the columns of text using metallic silver ink with the size 2½ nib.

9 Add the final decoration at the bottom of the right-hand column with the fine silver pen.

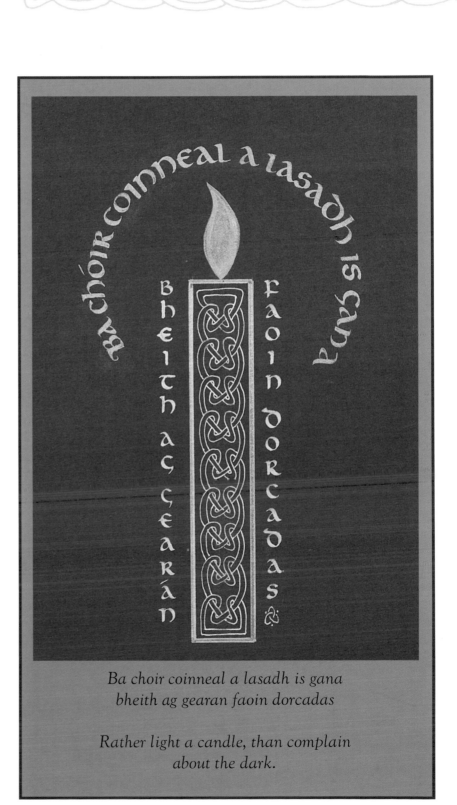

Ba choir coinneal a lasadh is gana bheith ag gearan faoin dorcadas

Rather light a candle, than complain about the dark.

Monogram Lampshade

Here is an inventive idea for your home – a stamped monogram lampshade with either

your initials, or the initials of you and that special person in your life, entwined.

Introducing the craft skill of cutting a lino board, you will learn to make a stamp which

can be used on a number of objects, such as personalized stationery.

Materials

Lino board
Cutting board and
  craft knife
30cm (12in) metal ruler
Cartridge paper
Tracing paper
H and 2B pencils
Lino-cutting tools
  and handle
Fabric paints – blue,
  violet, silver and yellow
Size 1 and 3 brushes
Palette
Water jar
Masking tape
Neutral coloured
  lampshade

1 Cut the lino board into smaller pieces with a craft knife and metal-edged ruler. Make sure it is big enough to take your design with a margin of 1cm (½in) to the edge of the lino board.

2 Trace the initials from the alphabet (page 22). Alternatively, write your own on a sheet of cartridge paper and trace from this. Then, because the stencil is a reversed image, carbonize the front of the design and place it upside down on the lino board before transferring the design with a hard pencil. Repeat with the triskele design (page 117).

3 Begin cutting the pattern by making a single incision along the pencil lines with a craft knife. Ensure the tip of the blade goes through the hard surface about halfway to the hessian backing.

4 Place the small V-shaped blade into the handle of the lino-cutting tool and cut very slowly and carefully along the outside of the pencil lines. Use firm pressure but do not cut too deeply at this stage. Cut slowly all the way round the design – a mistake at this stage will ruin the stencil.

5 Swap the V-shaped blade for a wide curved blade to remove the mass of excess lino around the stamp. You need to take out all the lino board right to the edges. Try to have clean cut lines as the stamp will work much better. Next, cut off the corners of the stamp so that it fits comfortably into the hand.

To use the lino-cutting tool effectively, press the base of the wooden handle into the palm of the hand and wrap your fingers around it so that you have a firm but comfortable grip.

6 Now mix the fabric paints with a little silver paint to give them some sheen. Take the size 3 brush and place some purple in the palette, adding only a drop of water and some of the silver paint. Mix together. Repeat with the blue and yellow colours, mixing each well.

7 Use the size 1 brush to paint the colours onto the initials. Apply a little of the blue paint and then the purple evenly to the cut initials, using one colour for each letter.

8 Now print onto the lampshade. Hold the inside of the lamp with your left hand as a support and press firmly straight onto the shade with your right hand, keeping the stamp as flat as possible to the surface.

9 Reapply the two paint colours each time you use the stamp. Lift it away smoothly, making sure not to smudge the initials you have just stamped.

Tip

Use a round-handled craft knife to cut the lino as it is more difficult to create smooth corners with a straight-bladed knife – and also more uncomfortable on the hand.

10 Repeat this process with the triskele design, mixing some yellow with a little silver. Try not to get the paint in between the circle cut lines. Stamp in the spaces left between the initials until the lampshade is complete.

Wooden Christening Plaque

This unusual christening plaque uses metallic inks painted on a round wooden plaque,

and a Celtic knot panel to illustrate eternity with no beginning or end.

The Gaelic word 'Failte' means 'welcome'.

Materials

Wooden plaque
   (20cm/8in)
Fine sandpaper
Matt varnish
Flat varnish brush
Tracing paper
H and 2B pencils
Size 0 brush
Pearlized yellow, violet
   and green ink
Fine line black pen
30cm (12in) ruler
Cartridge paper
Compass
Pen holder
Size 1 and 2 nibs
2 ink reservoirs

1 Before writing, sand down the front of the plaque and varnish it before leaving it overnight to dry. Mark the outline of the plaque on a sheet of tracing paper then trace the template of the round Celtic knot border (page 123), enlarging or reducing its size to fit if necessary.

2 Carbonize the back with the 2B pencil then stick in place with masking tape and use the H pencil to go over all the border.

3 Now take a size 0 brush and paint the unknotted ribbon with yellow pearlized ink, taking care to go over and under the other ribbons in turn. Make sure you keep stirring the ink to mix it well during the painting. Follow with the violet, and then the green ink. Allow to dry.

4 Go around all the borders with the fine line marker pen to emphasize the colours, again checking the over and under movement of the Celtic design.

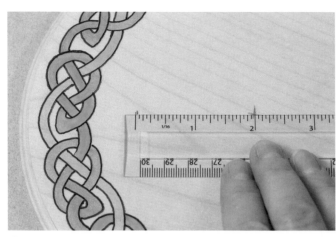

5 Find the centre point on the plaque and mark it with a cross. Draw a small pencil line with the 2B pencil to a point 2cm (³/₄in) from the border and measure this distance.

6 Now take a sheet of cartridge paper and draw a circle with a compass of the same radius as previously measured. Then, with a pen and a size 1 nib, draw 4½ pen widths down from the pencil line and draw a second circle with the compass to create a circular writing stave.

7 Use the 2B pencil to practise the spacing of the Half-uncial lettering. Make the two initial letters – A and F – slightly larger than the rest. Also create a flat stave with the size 2 nib and practise writing the date.

8 Repeat the previous step on the plaque, drawing in the stave and lettering in pencil, taking care to centre both words in relation to the horizontal date line.

9 Now write the words in ink using the size 1 nib and reservoir, ensuring the initial letters are slightly larger than the rest. Allow to dry before writing the date with the size 2 nib. Again, allow to dry.

10 Trace the templates of the two animal decorations (page 123) and carbonize as before, placing them on top of two of the letters.

11 Draw the animals in with the fine line black pen and add decoration to some of the other letters.

12 Paint the animals with coloured ink and also add colour to some of the letters at this stage. To finish, rubrify the two initial letters using the fine line black pen, erase any remaining pencil marks and varnish the plaque.

Zoomorphic Letter

Based on the Irish Half-uncial alphabet dating from the fine manuscript books of the

seventh and eighth centuries, this illuminated letter B incorporates a traditional animal

design, known as a zoomorphic.

1 Fold the card in half lengthways then find the centre of the card by lightly drawing lines down and across the card with the soft pencil.

2 Transfer your letter B from the template (page 118) onto a sheet of tracing paper, or draw your own designed letter. Turn it over and carbonize the back with a soft pencil. Turning it right way round, centre the letter on the card using the pencil lines to guide you and stick it down with masking tape.

Materials

Sheet of off-white card

30cm (12in) ruler

H and 2B pencils

Tracing paper

Masking tape

Eraser

Gouache colours

Palette

Water jar

Gum arabic

Size 1 brush

Fine line black pen

Fine line red pen

3 With a hard pencil go over the letter, transferring the design to the card.

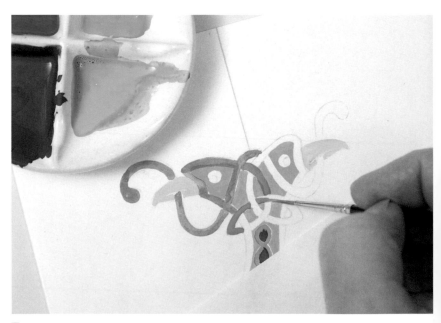

4 Carefully rub out the pencil cross with an eraser before redrawing any of the design that has also been removed.

5 Now paint the letter using the gouache colours. Mix a little paint in the palette with a drop of gum arabic and water until it is the consistency of single cream. Use the size 0 brush to paint along the pencil lines then fill in the rest of the colour. Work in this method for each section and each colour.

6 When each colour is dry, mix the next and work into the design. Use progressively darker colours so that any mistakes can be hidden by the neighbouring shade.

7 Finish the colouring by filling in the blue ribbon that loops around the bird design.

8 Outline the design with the fine line black pen to solidify the colours and make each section stand out.

9 When outlining the knotwork, take special care to ensure that the ribbon never goes over or under two consecutive elements. If necessary have the template to hand as a guide.

10 To finish, add either red or black dots around the outer edge of the letter with a fine line pen.

Rainbow Alphabet Book

This little concertina alphabet book will help children learn their letters in a fun way.

Adding gouache to the pen nib without washing each previous colour off the nib creates

a smooth flow of colour from page to page.

1 Cut an A3 sheet into six strips each 7.5cm (3in) wide. Find the position of the letters by drawing lines along the length of the strip 2cm (¾in) from top and bottom then mark divisions every 7.5cm (3in). Now measure 2cm (¾in) on both sides of these divisions, creating squares for each letter.

Materials

Cream parchment card
30cm (12in) ruler
Cutting board
Craft knife
Automatic pen
Gouache colour – scarlet,
    ultramarine, bright green,
    yellow, purple and white
Large palette
Water jar
Gum arabic
Size 1, 2 and 3 brushes
PVA glue
Tracing paper
3 x 50cm (20in) ribbon
Marbled paper
H and 2B pencils
Fine line black pen

2 The squares will not reach along the length of the strip so mark 2.5cm (1in) from the end of the last letter space and draw a line, then cut along it with a craft knife.

3 Start painting in the third space. Add scarlet paint to the automatic pen with a paintbrush, stroking the brush tip across the V shape, filling the inside of the pen with paint.

4 Let each letter fill the square. For the next letter (the 'B') add some yellow to the red gouache remaining in the automatic pen to create a mixed orange colour.

5 Apply more yellow gouache to the nib for the 'C' so that the colour is almost pure. Continue until all 26 letters have been painted.

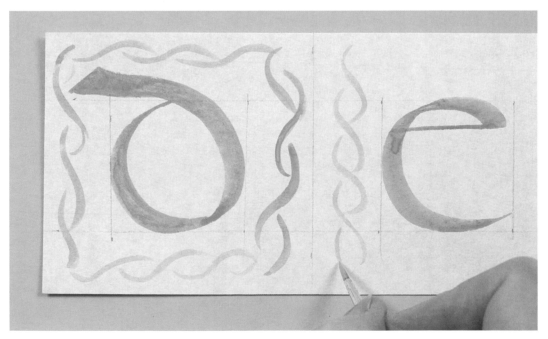

6 Use a size 1 paintbrush to add a border around each letter, freehand, matching the colour combinations of the letters.

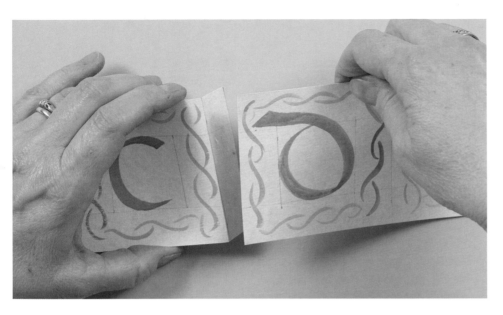

7 Fold over the end line and and cover it with PVA glue then stick the lengths of letters together. Concertina the long strip, folding over the card along the pencil lines.

8 When all the strips are connected fold the card into a concertina, pressing along the pencil lines that divide the letters.

9 To create the cover designs, trace the knotwork from the template (page 124) and carbonize the reverse, transferring the design onto marbled paper. Work heavily to ensure the pencil shows up on the marbled paper.

10 Go over the pencil on the marbled paper with a black pen then paint in the blocks of colour with a size 2 paintbrush.

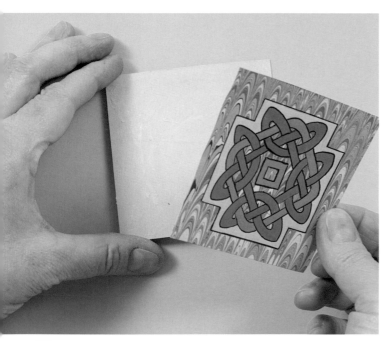

11 Use PVA glue to stick the marbled paper to a piece of card cut to the same size.

12 When it is dry cut a hole in the centre with a craft knife to enable the ribbons to be inserted.

13 Thread the three ribbons through the hole, flatten them and stick the ends down onto the back of the card then cover all of the card with glue.

14 Stick the marbled card onto the back of the concertina, so that the ribbons align with the concertina. Create a second marbled card without a hole or ribbons and stick it onto the front of the card. Tie the ribbon around the folded book.

Tip

Rather than making a book, you could display the strip of letters in a frame to decorate a child's bedroom wall.

Garden Seed Box

This inventive gift for seed collectors can be made from any size cardboard box and some

paper. On the top, it reads 'garden seed' in Gaelic, written in Irish Half-uncial script.

Around the lid in Latin are flower, herb and vegetable names.

Materials

15cm (6in) ruler
Cardboard box with lid
Green card in 2
    shades
Pinking shears
PVA glue
Green parchment card
Compass
White cartridge paper
Size 10 double-point nib
Pen holder
Turquoise ink
H and 2B pencils
Tracing paper
Size 0 brush
Brown and yellow inks
Fine line gold pen
Fine line black pen
Calligraphy felt tip
    gold pen
Eraser

1 Measure the box lid and cut one of the sheets of green card to fit. Use the decorative scissors to cut around the edge, allowing a little of the box edge to show all round. Place onto the lid and stick down with PVA glue. Cut the other green card slightly smaller and stick down on top. Measure the parchment writing card slightly smaller than the last and cut to fit but do not stick it down yet.

2 Find the middle of the parchment by measuring across and down the card and drawing one line across and one down to find the centre point. Create the top curved writing line by placing the compass onto the bottom of the middle line and drawing a semicircle about 2.5cm (1in) from the top of the card.

3 Use the compass at the same setting to draw a similar curve on the cartridge practice paper. Draw a 4½ pen-width stave with the size 10 double-point nib using turquoise ink. Recalibrate the compass and draw a second curve from the bottom of the stave, making sure the point is in exactly the same place.

4 Now practise writing the Gaelic word for garden, *gairdin*, keeping the letters upright along the writing line. Turn the paper as you move around the curve so that your writing is always upright.

5 Underneath draw a line and make a second 4½ pen-width stave, adding a pencil writing line. Practise writing the word *siol*, meaning seed.

6 On the parchment card add the curved writing line at the top by using the compass spread to the same distance as on the practice sheet, placing the point in the same place as in Step 2. Add the straight writing line 2.5cm (1in) up from the bottom of the card. Measure the height of the writing line on the practice sheet and replicate this height on the card.

7 Go back to your practice sheet and measure the length of the writing lines and transfer the start point measurement to the green parchment card.

8 Write the card using the turquoise ink and double-point nib, taking care to centre the writing along the curved line.

9 Draw the seed shapes, trace the Celtic knot motif from the template (page 117), carbonize the back and transfer it onto the middle of the box lid with a hard pencil.

10 Now use a fine brush to paint the seeds with a variety of shades of brown ink and the Celtic motif with turquoise ink.

11 Fill in the open spaces between the lines of letters and the centre of the Celtic motif with a gold fine line pen then outline the seeds with a fine line black pen.

12 Cut 4 squares of parchment card 5cm (2in) square. Trace the Celtic knot design from the tracing paper onto all four pieces. Draw the lines with turquoise ink and fill in with the gold fine line pen. Finally, cut the edges with the decorative scissors and stick the card onto the box sides.

13 Take the gold calligraphy permanent felt tip pen and write the Latin names of plants all the way round the side of the lid, forming a border of words. It does not matter if the word does not finish at the end of the line, just continue to write on the next side of the lid until all is covered.

14 To finish, stick the green parchment card onto the lid on top of the other green shades of card.

Celtic Jewellery Box

The angular square letters on the lid of the box read 'jewellery' in Gaelic and are painted

similarly to the letters in the Irish Book of Kells. Celtic jewellery adorns the box, echoing

ancient Celtic designs – choose any you like from the templates on page 116.

1 Prepare the box by smoothing the lid along the grain with fine sandpaper and varnishing it using long strokes with the flat brush. Allow it to dry overnight. Transfer the decorations and words from the template (page 116) onto tracing paper and cut them out.

2 Carbonize the back of the lettering with the soft pencil before sticking it to the box lid with masking tape and transferring the design with a hard pencil.

Materials

Wooden box

Fine sandpaper

Matt clear varnish

Soft flat varnish brush

Tracing paper

H and 2B pencils

Masking tape

Fine line black pen

30cm (12in) ruler

Gouache colour – red,
    blue, green, yellow,
    purple, gold and silver

Eraser

Size 1 and 3 brushes

White spirit

Palette

Water jar

3 Also carbonize the decorations and place them in turn around the lettering, then transfer them to the lid with a hard pencil.

4 Use the fine line black pen to go over all the pencil lines you have transferred. At this stage incorporate the Celtic jewellery by placing some of it behind the lettering. Remove any pencil lines.

5 Add some gouache colour to the word, starting with the yellow background to the lettering. First mark a line alongside the pen line then fill in with colour.

6 Continue with the green and red colours of the letters. Let each stage dry before starting the next colour.

7 Next, paint in the knotwork corners and motifs with coloured gouache before finally going around the word panel with two rows of red dots. Also go round the corner designs with a black fine line pen. Finally, varnish the box to seal the work.

You can use the template as a starting point or, alternatively, design your own decoration on a sheet of paper. When you are happy with the design use it like any of the templates included in this book.

Tip

When tracing intricate designs don't attempt to copy every tiny detail. Once you have transferred the main outline to the box, have the original template to hand and copy the details when highlighting the lines with the fine line pen.

Rune Stones

Rune stones were used many centuries ago by the people of Scandinavia, who believed

that they held special powers of protection when carried by the owner. Try painting one

of the symbols that you are especially drawn to, to be carried as a talisman.

Materials

White card for practice
Size 1 brush
Enamel paints – red, light
   blue, yellow, green,
   purple and dark blue
25 white pebbles
White spirit

1 Using enamel paint and the size 1 brush, practise painting the runes on the white card. Stir the paint well then work freehand with no ruling up. Start by painting the upright strokes, then the diagonal strokes.

2 Wash the stones in soapy water and allow them to dry before you begin painting the symbols. Use one colour to paint four of the runes. Again, paint the upright strokes first, then the diagonal lines.

Tips

● As all pebbles are different shapes and sizes use all the available space on the surface of the stones.

● Paint at least two coats of lighter colours, waiting for them to dry before applying the next coat.

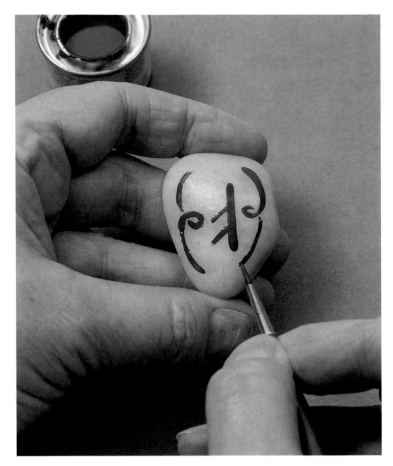

3 Then paint the side decoration, also freehand. Start the right-hand side decoration at the top, painting down the pebble to the bottom. Then turn the pebble round and paint the other side so that you always turn the brush clockwise.

4 Wash the brush in white spirit, and then do the same with each colour until you have painted all the stones. Leave for at least 24 hours before handling them.

Templates

The following pages include some of the more complicated Celtic designs and decorations. Enlarge these templates to the size you require on a photocopier then trace and transfer them to your project, inserting your own lettering where necessary.

Celtic Jewellery Box, page 110

Uncial Place Card, page 64

Wishing Stone, page 40

Wooden Picture Frame, page
50 and Garden Seed Box,
page 104

Monogram Lampshade, page 86

Gaelic House–Blessing Card, page 46

Wooden Picture Frame, page 50

Zoomorphic Letter, page 94

Illuminated Letter R, page 56

Ceilidh Invitation, page 67

Chinese Proverb, page 82

Ex Libris Book Plate, page 80

Ceilidh Invitation, page 67

Name Plaque on Wood, page 42

Celtic Bookmark, page 78

Wooden Christening Plaque, page 90

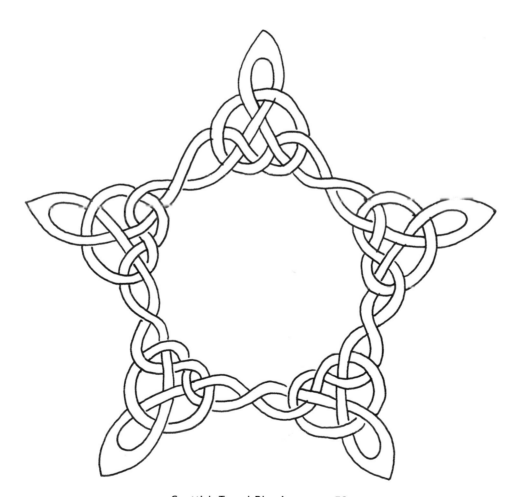

Scottish Travel Blessing, page 52

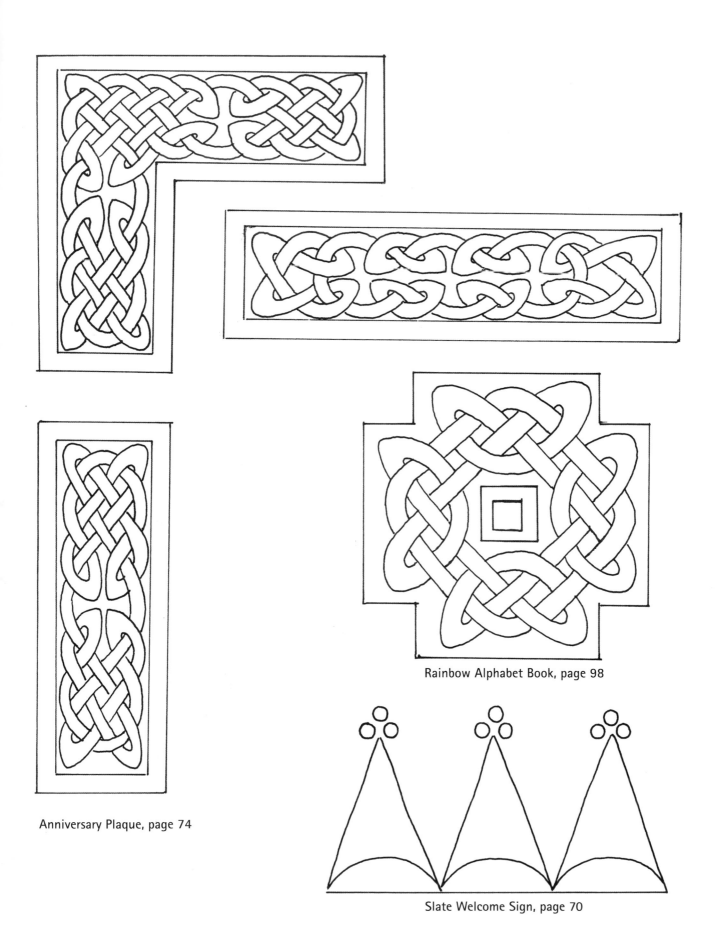

Anniversary Plaque, page 74

Rainbow Alphabet Book, page 98

Slate Welcome Sign, page 70

Anniversary Plaque, page 74

Suppliers and Websites

There are many suppliers specializing in the calligrapher's mainstays: papers, pens, nibs, brushes and inks. Alternatively, general art stores will be able to supply you with the majority of your materials, and all are available through an ever-growing number of internet-based distributors.

Suppliers

Brackendale Arts
1 Sparvell Way
Camberley, Surrey GY15 3SF
United Kingdom
Tel/Fax: +44 (0)1276 681344
http://www.brackendalearts.co.uk
Wide range of calligraphy equipment.

L. Cornelissen & Son
105 Great Russell Street
London WC1B 3RY
United Kingdom
Tel: +44 (0)20 7636 2045
http://www.cornelissen.com
Calligraphy materials, brushes and pigment powder. Ships abroad.

Falkiner Fine Papers
76 Southampton Row
London WC1B 4AR
United Kingdom
Tel: +44 (0)20 7831 1151
A wide range of specialist paper, calligraphy and bookbinding supplies.

Japan Centre
212 Piccadilly
London W1J 9HG
United Kingdom
Tel: +44 (0)20 7255 8260
http://www.japancentre.com
Japanese paper specialists.

Manuscript Pen Company Ltd.
Highley Nr Bridgnorth
Shropshire WV16 6NN
United Kingdom
Tel: +44 (0)1746 861236
Fax: +44 (0)1746 862737
http://www.calligraphy.co.uk
For supplies not widely available in U.S. Ships abroad.

Scribblers
12 Witney Road
Pakefield, Lowestoft
Suffolk, NR33 7AW
United Kingdom
Tel: +44 (0)1502 562392
http://www.scribblers.co.uk
Calligraphy supplies and the unique X-Height Calculator. Ships abroad.

Websites

A search on the Internet will yield a vast wealth of resources on calligraphy, from classes and workshops to suppliers and publications.

http://www.cynscribe.com
A good place to start your search is with this online directory of more than 1,000 calligraphy links.

http://www.winsornewton.com
One of the most comprehensive ranges of all types of calligraphy equipment, available worldwide.

http://www.tigon-crafts.co.uk
Information about the Celtic alphabets from author Fiona Graham-Flynn.

Index

Acknowledgements

I would like to dedicate *The Simple Art of Celtic Calligraphy* to the following people: my dear husband, Christopher, whose constant love, patience, and support gave me the courage to write this book, to my parents John and Gwen Graham, who are with me in spirit and always believed in the talent I was given, to my dear son Sam and, lastly, my grandchildren, Lucy and Louis, who always show an interest in my calligraphy. I hope one day they may come to learn by it.

My thanks go to my uncle, Gerald Flynn, and friends in Limerick, for all their kind help with the Gaelic translations.

I would also like to say thank you to CICO Books for giving me the opportunity to write this book – it means so much to me.

Picture Credits

Page 6 (bottom): The Board of Trinity College, Dublin, Ireland/The Bridgeman Art Library
Page 7: British Library Board/The Bridgeman Art Library